LET'S GO ESPAÑOL!

Spanish Activities
Book 1

Created by:
Señora Dillon

LET'S TACO-BOUT NUMBERS!

Color each taco. Practice counting in Spanish as you go!

1 uno	2 dos	3 tres
4 cuatro	5 cinco	6 seis
7 siete	8 ocho	9 nueve

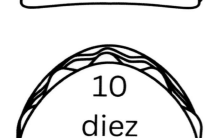  

10 diez	11 once	12 doce

Los Colores

Spanish Color	Pronunciation	Translation
rojo	RO-hoh	red
azul	ah-SOOL	blue
verde	VAIR-day	green
café	kah-FAY	brown
blanco	BLAHN-koh	white
rosado	ros-AH-do	pink
anaranjado	ah-nah-ran-HA-do	orange
morado	moor-AH-do	purple
gris	GREESS	gray
amarillo	AH-mah-REE-yoh	yellow
negro	NAY-groh	black

Mi Mochila

What's in your backpack? Look at the school supplies on the next page. Draw each school supply on the backpack and label in Spanish.

cuaderno

libro

regla

tijeras

papel

pegamento

crayon

lapiz

Festive Patterns

Can you complete each pattern? Draw a line from the picture below to the box where it belongs to continue that pattern.

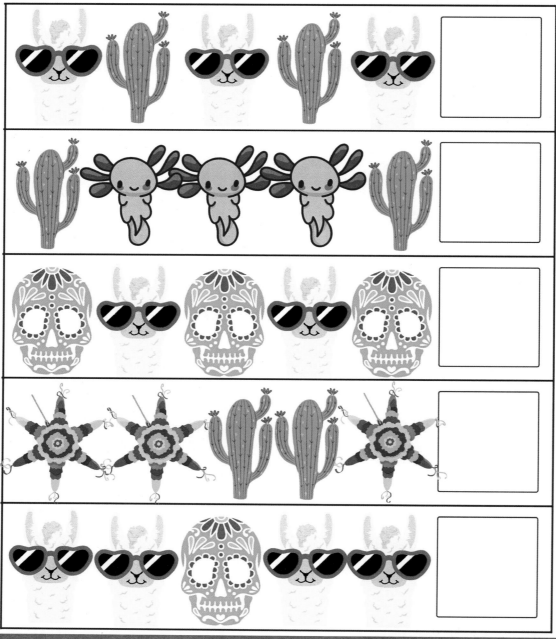

A	T	R	E	S	P	W	I	M	K	D
O	G	M	V	N	S	U	X	A	G	O
Q	H	J	V	D	O	S	W	J	I	C
T	V	G	G	T	D	E	T	I	J	E
C	Z	J	D	Q	V	I	A	J	M	O
S	I	E	T	E	Q	S	E	G	P	y
G	O	N	U	F	X	F	X	Z	X	S
G	P	N	C	U	A	T	R	O	K	A
V	J	Q	W	O	U	G	H	S	C	y
K	A	C	S	N	N	C	B	H	U	S
U	J	O	y	O	O	N	C	E	U	V

uno	dos	tres
cuatro	cinco	seis
siete	ocho	nueve
diez	once	doce

Beach Day

- Color the sun amarillo.
- Color the big cloud azul. Leave the small cloud blanco.
- Color the jumping dolphin gris.
- Color the beach chair rojo.
- Color the umbrella in different colores.
- Color the big coconut tree verde.
- Color the sand castle cafe.
- Color the kids' clothes anaranjado.
- Color the duck float amarillo.
- Color the sandals morado.

COLOR THE SUGAR SKULL

Guess the Job

Read the clues and guess the job. Use the pictures at the bottom to help you write the correct Spanish answer in each box.

I help put out fires and save people. I'm a...

I teach children. I work at a school. I'm a...

I make delicious dishes. I work in a kitchen. I'm a...

I take care of you when you are sick. I work at a hospital. I'm a...

maestra

cocinero

bombero

doctora

Write a postcard to a friend or family member! Try to use 3-5 Spanish words in your writing!

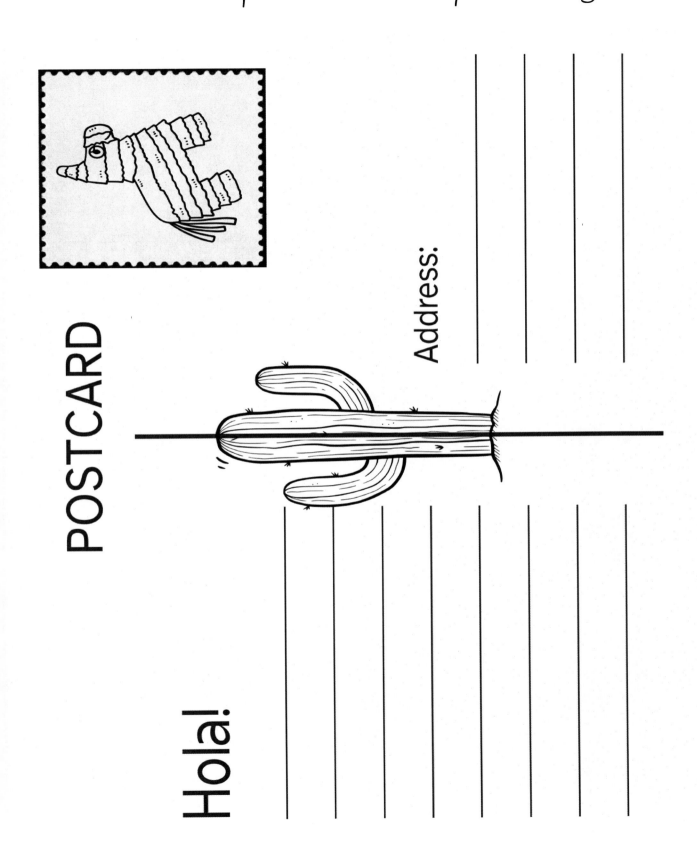

POSTCARD

Hola!

Address:

LAS PALETAS – THE POPSICLES

Color the popsicles below using the Spanish colors for each number.

1 blanco   **3** rosado   **5** rojo

2 azul   **4** verde   **6** amarillo

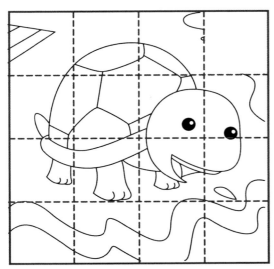

Finish drawing la tortuga

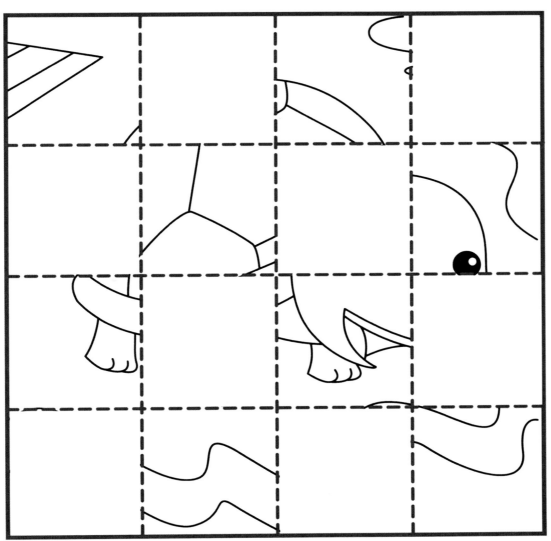

LOS ANIMALES

WRITING PRACTICE

Copy each Spanish animal word in the box below.

conejo

vaca

elefante

jirafa

cebra

tigre

león

ballena

zorro

camello

Picture This

Color each picture and think good thoughts!

Arco iris – Rainbow

Feliz – Happy

Corazón – Heart

Paz – Peace

Flor – Flower

SLOTH MAZE

Can you help the baby sloth find its mom?

COLOR

I Spy Cinco de Mayo

1. Color then count each set of pictures you find.
2. Write the number beside each picture on the grid.
3. See if you can say each of these numbers in Spanish.

flamenco Color by Number

Use the key at the bottom of the page to color the picture.

1. rosado   2. azul   3. verde
4. gris   5. cafe   6. negro

Check off each one as you find it outside!
Then color the pictures!

NATURE WALK
SCAVENGER HUNT

hoja | tronco | mariposa

flor | ardilla | mariquita

pájaro | roca | hormiga

hongo | bellota | árbol

I E A M A R I L L O L O M X X

Y B C O L O R E S D O B L

V L X D A A X T Y B R U C

T A F K I C E X W N A V V

D N I F C R G R I S D C O

C C H D N O P A T X O A D

V O R W E I Z I G P K F V

Y T V K H R O J O M E E F

I M W V I I N O C H N R A

F T C S X S V E R D E D Z

V O J G Q F Y X E W G L U

R O S A D O Y L U F R M L

H C H K K B V Z H Y O N P

acro iris	rojo	azul
verde	gris	cafe
amarillo	colores	blanco
negro	rosado	morado

LA MARIPOSA

Use the grid to help you draw the other side of the buttefly, then color symmetrically:

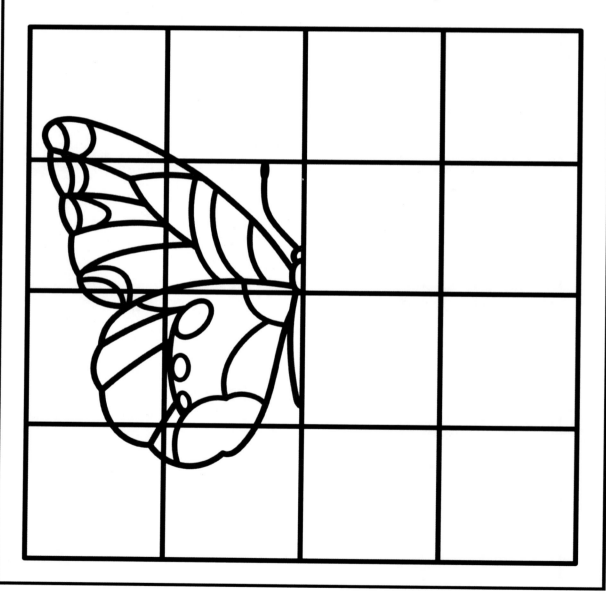

Feed the llama by helping
him get to the hay!

La Cara - The Face

Have fun and draw the body parts below on the face!

ojos

nariz

boca

HOW MANY SCHOOL SUPPLIES?

Count the school supplies and write the Spanish number in the boxes. Then color the pictures.

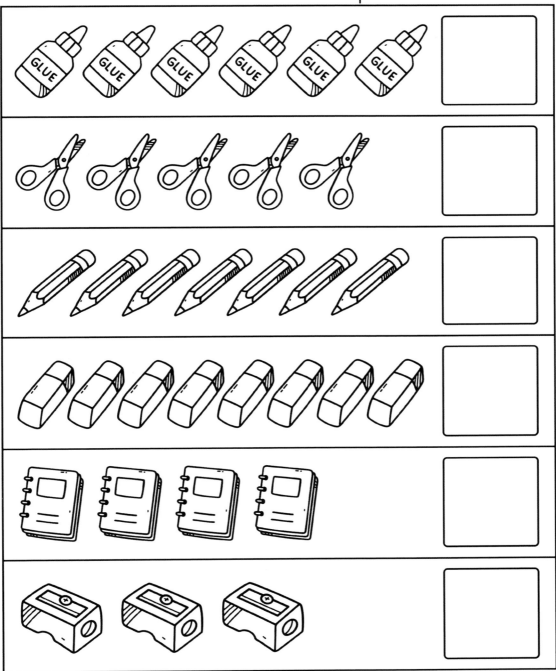

The sun is commonly seen in Mexican art. Color the sol above! Get creative with your design. Label it: "El Sol - The Sun".

Write a postcard to a friend or family member! Try to use 3-5 Spanish words in your writing!

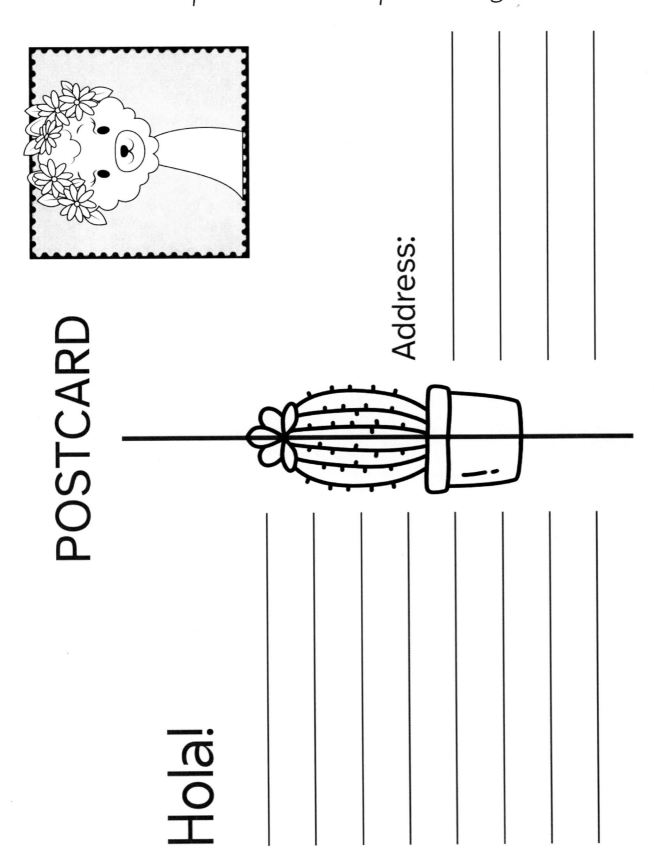

POSTCARD

Hola!

Address:

Color the clothing below so it is ready for your closet

camisa

zapatos

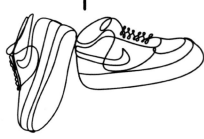

pantalones

COLOR THE PAPEL PICADO BELOW.

LAS ESTACIONES

Draw a picture for each season.

PRIMAVERA

VERANO

OTOÑO

INVIERNO

Let's Eat!

Draw each of these fruits below on the plate.
Then label in Spanish.

manzana

uvas

sandia

Taco Counting

Count the tacos in the boxes below and write the correct Spanish number in the space provided.

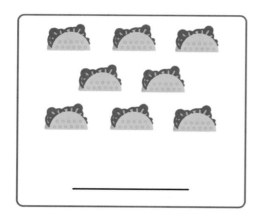

_____

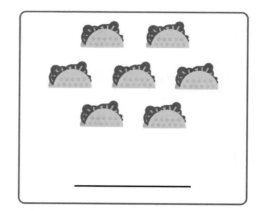

_____

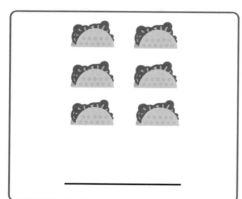

_____

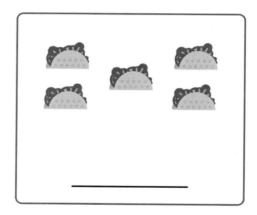

_____

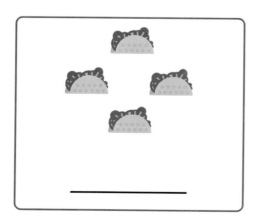

_____

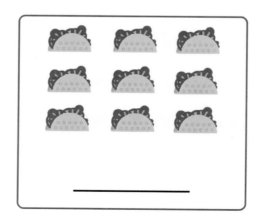

_____

color all the rectángulo objects!

COLOR EL TUCÁN

Did you know toucans live in Central and South America?

CINCO DE MAYO
Word Search

```
T P W H A S G Q I N
M A Y E M P U K H E
E R C N N U A I C R
M A M O R E G M A S
D D N C S V A G I R
M E X I C O M N R E
I H B S A R W A C
A D E U B A L A M N
L R R M P U E B L A
V I C T O R Y Z J D
```

May   tacos   music

dancers   mariachi   guacamole   Puebla

victory   Mexico   parade

AMIGOS STICK TOGETHER

COLOR THE GATO

1= verde   3= amarillo   5= morado

2= azul   4= anaranjado   6= rosado

HELP!

This armadillo lost his sombrero hat. Can you help him find it?

color all the triángulo objects!

LET'S WRITE!

Create an acrostic poem with the word SPANISH. See if you can use Spanish words or things that have to do with Hispanic culture. For example, P piñata.

S _____

P _____

A _____

N _____

I _____

S _____

H _____

LA ROPA - CLOTHING

Draw a hat on the person. Label it **gorro**. Draw mittens on the hands. Label them **mitones**. Draw boots on the feet. Label them **botas**. Also make sure to draw a face!

LA PLAYA - THE BEACH

Look at the pictures below and circle the differences.

COLOR

color all the círculo objects!

Let's Make Avocado Boats!

What You'll Need:
1 ripe avocado
¼ cup finely chopped celery
1 cup shredded or cubed cooked chicken
2 tablespoons mayonnaise

Before you begin, ask an adult to:
Cut the avocado in half.
Remove the pit.
Scoop out the avocado from the shell.
Set shells aside.
Finely chop the celery.

What to do:

Combine the celery, chicken, and mayonnaise in a bowl. Mix well.

Lightly mash the avocado with a potato masher or fork. Add it to the chicken mixture.

Fill each avocado "boat" with the mixture. Enjoy!

Wordsearch

Create your own wordsearch using Spanish words from this book!

Los Números

Fill in the missing Spanish numbers.

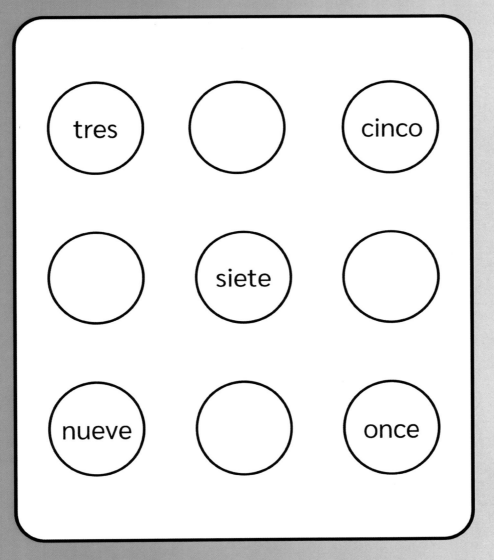

Color La Guitarra

LA ESCUELA - SCHOOL

COLOR ALL THE DIFFERENCES

Stay tuned...
more activity books to come!

Made in United States
North Haven, CT
16 October 2023

42800678R00029